LEARNING ABOUT
Animals

Catherine Veitch

Raintree

Chicago, Illinois

The author would like to dedicate this book to her mother, Jacqueline Veitch, who inspired her with a love of nature.

© 2014 Raintree
an imprint of Capstone Global Library, LLC
Chicago, Illinois
capstonepub.com

Edited by Dan Nunn, Rebecca Rissman, and Sian Smith
Designed by Joanna Hinton-Malivoire
Picture research by Mica Brancic
Production by Sophia Argyris
Originated by Capstone Global Library Ltd

Library of Congress Cataloging-in-Publication Data
Veitch, Catherine.
Learning about animals / Catherine Veitch.
pages cm.—(The natural world)
 Includes bibliographical references and index.
ISBN 978-1-4109-5404-6 (hardback)
ISBN 978-1-4109-5409-1 (paperback)
1. Animals—Juvenile literature. I. Title.
 QL49.V368 2014

 590—dc23   2012049395

Image Credits

Alamy: Avico Ltd, 18, 23; Avalon: NHPA/Stephen Dalton, 16, 24; Shutterstock: Anthony Shaw Photography, cover, Cathy Keifer, 6, 22, Christian Mueller, 17, Dmitry Kalinovsky, 12, Eduard Kyslynskyy, 15, Frantisek Czanner, 19, Herbert Kratky, 13, Irina Tischenko, 11, 22, 23, kool99, 12, 23, Mary Lane, 20 (inset), Mogens Trolle, 21, 23, PaulShlykov, 5 (inset), Peter Krejzl, 9, 22, REDSTARSTUDIO, 5, Reinhold Leitner, 20, 24, Sarel, back cover, 7, Sebastian Duda, 14 (all), 24, sergioboccardo, 21 (inset), Volodymyr Burdiak, 10, 22, Whytock, 4, worldswildlifewonders, 8, 23

We would like to thank Michael Bright for his invaluable help in the preparation of this book.

Every effort has been made to contact copyright holders of any material reproduced in this book. Any omissions will be rectified in subsequent printings if notice is given to the publisher.

Contents

Anteater...........................4
Cat 5
Chameleon 6
Crab 7
Crocodile 8
Deer 9
Duck 10
Fish 11
Goat 12
Hare 13
Hedgehog 14
Mouse 15
Owl 16
Robin 17
Sheep 18
Squirrel 19
Tortoise 20
Zebra 21
Picture Glossary 22
Notes for Parents and Teachers ...24

Anteater

Cat

5

Chameleon

Crab

Crocodile

Deer

Duck

Fish

Goat

Hare

Hedgehog

Mouse

Owl

16

Robin

Sheep

Squirrel

Tortoise

Zebra

Picture Glossary

antlers hard parts on an animal's head that look like branches. Animals can use antlers to fight or protect themselves.

beak hard part of a bird's mouth. Beaks can be different shapes, and they are used to help birds eat.

crest skin or feathers that stick up on top of an animal's head

fin part of a fish that helps the fish move through the water

gill part of a fish that helps the fish breathe

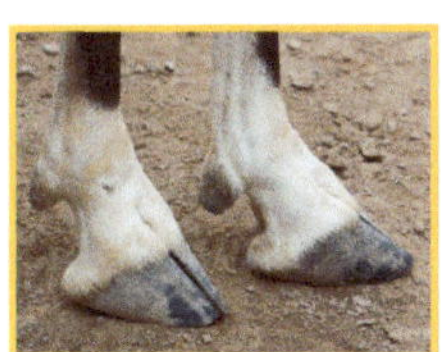

hoof hard part of the foot of some animals. Horses and goats have hooves.

horn hard, pointed part that grows out of an animal's head. Sheep and goats have horns.

mane hair that grows on the necks of animals such as zebras, horses, or lions

scales small, hard, overlapping parts that cover the skin of fish and reptiles

shell a hard body covering. Many animals with shells can hide inside them so that other animals cannot hurt them.

snout mouth and nose of some animals. A hedgehog has a snout.

spines stiff spikes. Spines can help keep animals safe from other animals that want to eat them.

talon long, sharp, hooked claw on the foot of an eagle or another bird. Talons are used to catch and carry things.

Notes for Parents and Teachers

- Go on a trip to a zoo. Take this book along, and ask the children to spot some of the animals shown in the book. Encourage the children to sketch or photograph what they see. Can they label the animals and animal parts?
- Use the images and labels to make a class book. Discuss the body parts of different animals and what the animals might use them for.